Science Experiments

WITH

SIMPLE
MACHINES

Sally Nankivell-Aston
and Dorothy Jackson

W
FRANKLIN WATTS

A Division of Scholastic Inc.

NEW YORK • TORONTO • LONDON • AUCKLAND • SYDNEY
MEXICO CITY • NEW DELHI • HONG KONG
DANBURY, CONNECTICUT

Acknowledgements: Cover Steve Shott;
AKG Photos, London p. 15br (Tbilissi, State Museum
of Georgia); James Davis Travel Photography p. 4cr;
Eye Ubiquitous pp. 6br (G. Daniels), 23tr (Andy
Butler); Leslie Garland Picture Library pp. 4cl, 25r
(Vincent Lowe); Robert Harding Picture Library pp.
17cl (R. Ashworth), 18br; The Stock Market p. 12br (T.
Stewart); Tony Stone Images pp. 5br (Don Smetzer),
13bl (Amwell), 27br (Joe Cornish).
Thanks, too, to our models: Troy Allick,
Shaheen Amirhosseini, Katie Appleby,
Shaun Cook, Stacie Damps, Stephanie Gharu,
Gabrielle Locke, James Moller and Joe Wood.

Series editor: Rachel Cooke; Designer: Mo Choy
Picture research: Susan Mennell; Photography: Ray
Moller, unless otherwise acknowledged

First published in 2000 by Franklin Watts

First American edition 2000 by Franklin Watts
A Division of Scholastic Inc.
557 Broadway, New York, NY 10012

Library of Congress Cataloging-in-Publication Data

Nankivell-Aston, Sally.
   Science experiments with simple machines/Sally
Nankivell-Aston and Dorothy Jackson.--1st American ed.
     p.cm
   Includes index.
   Summary: Explores properties of simple machines
through experiments, using material that is readily
available both in homes and schools.
   ISBN 0-531-14579-4 (library ed.) 0-531-15445-9 (pbk.)
    1. Simple machines--Experiments--Juvenile literature. [1.
Simple machines--Experiments. 2. Experiments.] I. Jackson,
Dorothy (Dorothy M.) III. Title.

TJ147 .N34 2000
621.8-078--dc21
                                        99-0544289

Contents

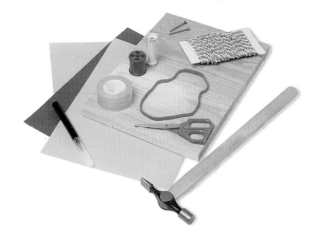

Machines All Around

WHICH OF THESE PICTURES show machines? All of them, in fact! How many machines can you spot? Machines can be complicated or simple, large or small, loud or quiet. We find them at home, at school, and in the workplace. Machines are everywhere! Can you think of the machines that you use in your daily life?

Be Amazed!

By doing the experiments in this book, you can learn some amazing things about machines — what they can do, why they are used, how they work, and how to make some for yourself. Some experiments may answer questions you already ask about machines. Some may make you think of more!

Look Closely!

Scientists ask lots of questions and observe carefully, which includes feeling as well as looking. When you do the experiments, look closely and keep a record of your results. Don't be upset if your predictions aren't correct, as scientists (and that includes you) learn a lot from unexpected results.

Be Careful!

Always make sure an adult knows that you are doing an experiment. Ask for help if you need to use sharp tools or heavy things. Follow the step-by-step instructions very carefully and remember — be a safe scientist!

All machines have one thing in common — they make a task (work) easier. The experiments in this book will help you find out about simple machines — levers, wheels and axles, pulleys and slopes, and the many different ways they can be used.

Lift Off!

Have you ever seen someone use a screwdriver to remove the lid from a paint can? The screwdriver is used as a simple machine called a lever. With levers, a push or pull force (called effort) is used to move something (the load), and the lever pivots (turns) at its fulcrum. There are three classes of levers. Find out about first-class levers in this experiment.

 You Will Need:
- a metal teaspoon
- a metal dessertspoon
- a metal tablespoon
- a fat felt-tip pen
- sticky putty
- a reasonably heavy box (e.g. toy box full of toys)

1 Put the pen on a hard-surfaced floor, about 1 inch (3 cm) away from the box, to act as a pivot. Stick it in place with sticky putty.

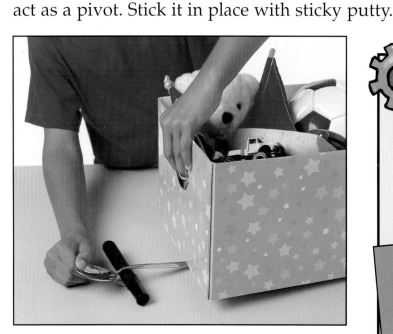

2 Put the end of the handle of the dessertspoon under the box, and rest the spoon over the pen.

In Action

Builders sometimes carry bricks in a hod. It is a type of lever — the bricks are the load, the builder's shoulder is the fulcrum, and his hand applies the effort.

3 Slowly push down on the spoon. Can you lift the box? Does it feel easy or hard to lift?

4 Now predict if the teaspoon or the tablespoon will make the job easier. Do a fair test to find out by repeating steps 1 to 3 with the different spoons. Which spoon makes the best lever?

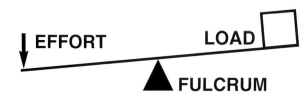

↓EFFORT   LOAD

▲FULCRUM

5 A first-class lever has its fulcrum between the effort and the load. The effort was the place where you pushed down, the fulcrum was the place where the lever pivoted, and the load was the object lifted. Where are these lever parts on the spoons?

Don't Stop There

● Using a long screwdriver as a lever, predict whether it is easier to open the lid on a can if you push at the end of the handle or nearer the lid. Test to find out.

● Place a broom over your shoulder, holding on tightly to the brush end. Ask a friend to hang a full gym bag on the broom handle, first near your shoulder, then near the end of the handle. In which position is your gym bag easier to carry?

A Robot With Levers

HAVE YOU EVER SEEN a puppet where you pull down on a string to make its arms (and sometimes legs!) move up? This type of toy is moved by levers. Make your own robot toy to find out how.

You Will Need:
- cardboard (e.g. from a cereal box)
- 4 paper fasteners
- 2 coins
- strong white yarn
- strong black yarn
- a wooden skewer
- felt pens

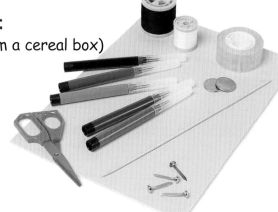

1 Use the cardboard to make a robot, following the measurements given on the diagram — you need four of Shape 2 for the arms and legs.

2 Mark the positions A, B, and C on each arm, and make holes at each point with the skewer. Tape a coin to the hand end of each arm.

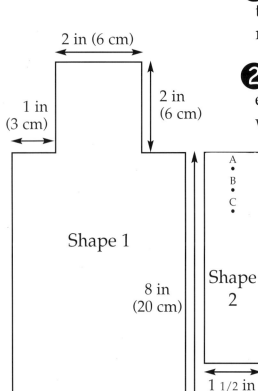

2 in (6 cm)

1 in (3 cm)

2 in (6 cm)

Shape 1

8 in (20 cm)

4 in (11 cm)

A
•
B
•
C
•

5 1/2 in (14 cm)

Shape 2

1 1/2 in (4 cm)

C B A

3 Put a paper fastener through each arm at position C; attach them to the body. Then use the other paper fasteners to attach the legs.

In Action

The arm on this mechanical toy uses a series of levers connected together. When you pull the two end levers together, the rest close up as well, making the arm longer.

4 Decorate the front of your robot.

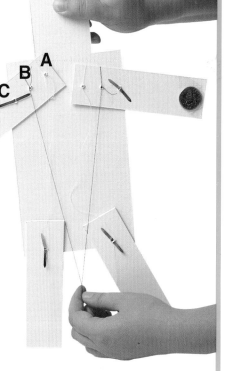

Keep Thinking

Can you label the effort, fulcrum, and load on each arm of your robot? Look back at pages 6 and 7 to see if this is a first-class lever.

5 Now thread a 12-inch (30-cm) length of white yarn through the hole at position A on each arm and tie in place. Pull the two threads down. What happens to the arms?

6 In the same way, thead 12-inch (30-cm) lengths of black yarn to each arm at position B.

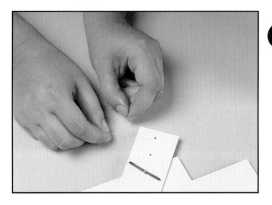

7 Pull the black threads down. Is it easier or harder to lift the arms this time? Which is the better position for the threads, A or B? Why?

Don't Stop There

Can you make the legs on your robot move as well? Think carefully about the best place to attach the yarn.

Shut That Door!

How many times today have you opened a door? A door is a second-class lever: the door hinges are the fulcrum, your push is the effort, and the door is the load. Where do you usually push on a door to open it? You probably push near the outside edge of the door, away from the hinged edge. Find out why in this experiment.

1 Stick three pieces of sticky putty to a door, level with its handle — one near the hinged edge (A), one in the middle (B), and one near the outer edge (C).

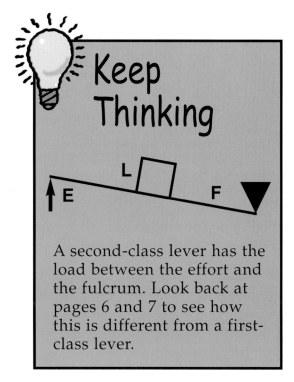

Keep Thinking

A second-class lever has the load between the effort and the fulcrum. Look back at pages 6 and 7 to see how this is different from a first-class lever.

2 Open the door, then shut it slowly by pushing on the piece of sticky putty at A, using only one finger. How does it feel? Is it easy or hard to shut the door?

❸ Now repeat the experiment, but this time shut the door by pushing at B. Remember to do the test in the same way to keep it fair. Does it feel easier or harder to shut the door?

In Action

There are many examples of second-class levers in everyday life, such as wheelbarrows and nutcrackers. Can you think of any more?

❹ Now do the test again, but this time at C. How easy was it this time? Which was the easiest place to push the door shut? Is it easiest when your push (effort) is farthest away from the hinges (the fulcrum)?

Don't Stop There

● Tape a piece of paper to the floor to cover the area the door swings over. Hold a felt pen to the bottom of the opened door, directly below point A. Shut the door holding the pen in position, so that it marks the paper as the door swings. Then measure the pen line using a piece of string.

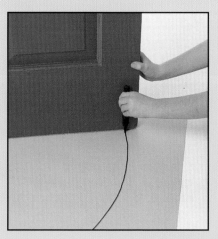

Repeat with the pen beneath point B and then C. Which line is the longest? When the door was easiest to shut, did you push for the longest or shortest distance?
● Look at cupboard handles and try them out. Is the handle always in the best position for opening the door?

Gone Fishing

D ID YOU KNOW THAT A FISHING rod is a type of lever? It is a third-class lever: The effort is between the fulcrum and the load. This experiment will tell you more about third-class levers.

✓ You Will Need:
- ✓ a 3-ft (1-m) bamboo cane
- ✓ a large paper clip
- ✓ 4 or 5 potatoes
- ✓ felt-tip pen
- ✓ colored tape
- ✓ 3-ft (1-m) string
- ✓ a plastic bag
- ✓ tape measure

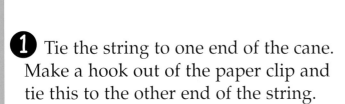

1 Tie the string to one end of the cane. Make a hook out of the paper clip and tie this to the other end of the string. You have now made your fishing rod!

2 Put marks at 10 in, 20 in, and 30 in (25 cm, 50 cm, and 75 cm) along the cane. Label the positions 1, 2, and 3, using the pen and colored tape.

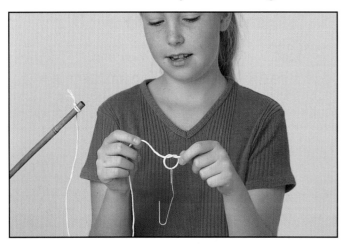

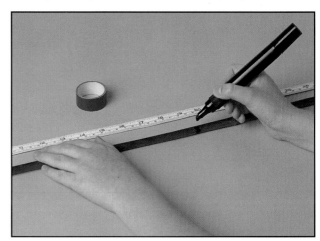

In Action

A deep-sea fisherman has a special harness that allows the rod to pivot so it acts as a fulcrum for the fishing line. This then allows him to use both his hands (the effort) to pull in a really heavy and powerful fish (the load).

3 Now put some potatoes in the bag, and put the bag on the hook.

4 Use your left hand to hold the end of the rod, and put your right hand at position 1 (10 in/25 cm). Try lifting your "catch" by raising the rod with your right hand. Keep your left hand steady, but allow the rod to pivot with your wrist. Does it feel easy or difficult?

5 Repeat the test with your right hand at position 2 and then 3. Which is the best place to pull up the rod to lift your load?

Don't Stop There

- Use a tennis racket to hit a ball. Your arm and the racket are working together as a lever. Part of your body is acting as a fulcrum. Can you think which?

- Use a broom to sweep up some dirt on the floor. Put one hand at the end of the handle. Where is the best place to put your other hand?

Keep Thinking

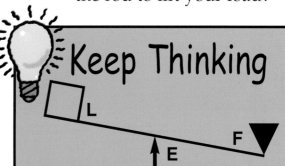

When you use your fishing line, your right hand pulls the potatoes up, so this hand provides the effort. Where is the fulcrum and where is the load? How is a third-class lever different from a first- or second-class lever? Look back at pages 6 and 7 and 10 and 11 for help.

Rolling Along

W<small>E USE WHEELS</small> to help things move along. They work with a rod called an axle. Try this experiment to find out how this type of machine makes a task easier.

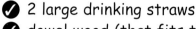
✔ You Will Need:
- ✔ a shoe box
- ✔ 4 wooden wheels
- ✔ a brick
- ✔ wooden rollers (e.g. round pencils)
- ✔ tape
- ✔ glue
- ✔ a saw
- ✔ 2 large drinking straws
- ✔ dowel wood (that fits through the straws and exactly into the wheels)

1 First make a cart. Cut the straws to the width of the shoe box. Tape them to the bottom of the box as shown.

⚙ In Action

The first wheels were made over 5,000 years ago. At first they were solid, made of wood or stone. Later, wheels with spokes were invented, which were much lighter. This bronze model of a chariot was made about 2,800 years ago. Its wheels have spokes. Do you think spokes made a chariot faster? Why?

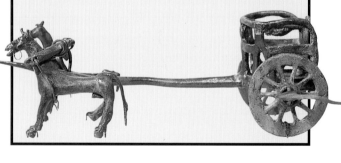

2 Ask an adult to help you saw two lengths of dowel wood 2 in (5 cm) longer than the width of the shoe box. These are your axles. Slide one through each straw and glue the wheels on each end. Allow to dry.

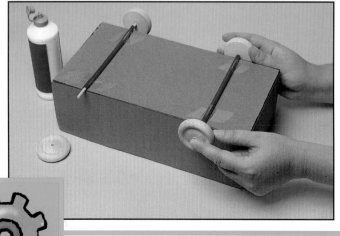

③ Now you are ready to experiment! First try pushing the brick along the floor, using only one finger.

④ Next, put the brick on the rollers and push it along in the same way. Does it feel easier or harder to move it?

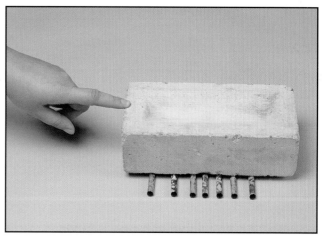

⑤ Finally, put the brick inside your shoe box cart. Push it along, as before. Do the wheels with axles make it easier or harder to move the brick along?

Don't Stop There

● Make rollers out of modeling clay and cut off slices. Look at the shape of the slices. Do you think they look like wheels?

● Cut out pictures of objects with wheel-and-axle mechanisms from magazines and catalogs. Make a collage to show the variety of ways in which we use wheels and axles in our daily lives. What tasks are made easier by wheels?

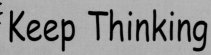

Keep Thinking

Some early wheels were made from slices of tree trunks. Where would you put the axle in such slices? Do you think they would have made good wheels?

Winch It Up!

Wheels and axles don't just help things roll along. You can use a wheel-and-axle to lift something up, too. This type of machine is called a winch. You may have seen a traditional well, where a winch is used to pull up a bucket of water. A winch can turn a small force into a large one. Find out more in this experiment.

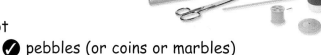

✓ You Will Need:
- ✓ 3 wooden wheels
- ✓ thread spool
- ✓ plastic cup or pot
- ✓ strong glue
- ✓ string
- ✓ pushpin
- ✓ scissors
- ✓ pebbles (or coins or marbles)
- ✓ 10-in (25-cm) length of dowel wood (that fits tightly through the wheels)
- ✓ cardboard box approx. 6 in x 8 in x 12 in (15 cm x 20 cm x 30 cm)

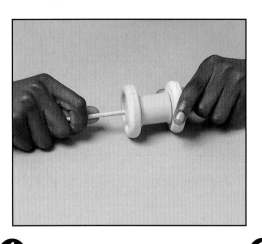

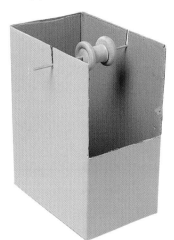

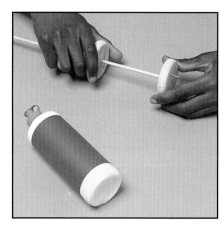

1 Glue a wheel to each end of the thread spool as shown. Slide this new large "wheel" onto the center of the dowel wood and stick it in position with glue.

2 Cut out the top half of the front of your box. Ask an adult to help you. Cut two slots in each side of the box, about 1 in (3 cm) deep and just wide enough to fit the dowel wood in. Drop the dowel wood into the slots.

3 Ask an adult to hammer the push-pin into the flat side of the third wheel. Stick it onto the dowel wood axle to use as a handle to turn the winch.

4 Use the string to make a handle for the plastic cup as shown. This is your bucket.

5 Attach the bucket to one end of a 16-in (40-cm) length of string. Tie the other end of the string tightly around the thread spool of the winch.

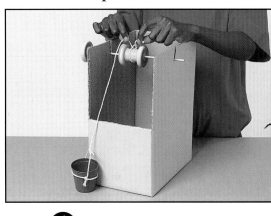

In Action

Winches on ships are used to pull up the anchor when they set sail. Can you think of other ways winches could be useful on a ship?

6 Fill your bucket with marbles and lift it by winding up the winch. Let the bucket down and lift it again, but this time by hand, right up to the same height. Which way of lifting feels easier?

Don't Stop There

- Use drinking straws cut lengthways to stop the axle from slipping through the slots, as in this picture. Can you think of other ways to improve your winch?

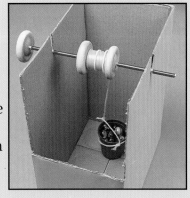

- Design a castle with a drawbridge that is pulled up and down by a winch (or winches).

Merry-Go-Round

WHEELS CAN BE USED IN machines to move a belt around and around — and the belt can then move other things. A bicycle works in this way, with the chain as the belt. These types of machines are called belt-driven machines. Make this toy merry-go-round to find out more.

SAFETY: Ask an adult to help you.

✔ **You Will Need:**
✔ a piece of wood about 8 in x 12 in x 3/4 in (20 cm x 30 cm x 2 cm)
✔ some pieces of thick paper
✔ a wide rubber band
✔ wide thread spool
✔ thin thread spool
✔ string
✔ tape
✔ a hammer
✔ 2 long nails

❶ Ask an adult to attach the thin thread spool near one edge of the piece of wood by hammering a nail through the hole in its center. Put a mark on the top of the spool with a pen.

❷ Attach the wide spool in the same way, positioning it a short distance from the first one so that the rubber band can stretch quite tightly around both the spools.

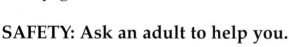

 In Action

The conveyor belt in this chocolate factory moves the chocolates along using a belt-driven machine.

3 To make the merry-go-round's central column, wrap some paper around the wider spool and secure it tightly with tape. The column needs to be about 4 in (10 cm) tall.

4 To make the top of the merry-go-round, cut out a circle about 2 3/4 in (7 cm) in diameter. Now cut out eight small horse shapes. Use tape to attach them with short lengths of thread (about 2 in/ 5 cm) around the edge of the paper circle.

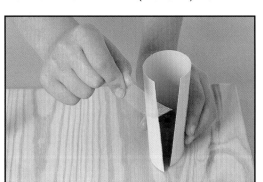

5 Stretch the rubber band over the thin spool and the merry-go-round column. Now attach the merry-go-round's top to the column with tape so the animals hang down.

6 Turn the thin spool around once. Use the mark on the top to help you. How far did the merry-go-round turn? How many turns of the thin spool do you need to make it turn around once? Does it turn in the same direction as the thin spool?

Don't Stop There

• Turn the thin spool around and around several times. Which moves faster — the thin spool or the merry-go-round?

• Take the rubber band off the thin wheel and twist it once. Then put it back over the spool. Turn the thin spool and watch what happens to the merry-go-round. Does it turn in the same direction as before?

Wheels With Teeth

Have you seen gears on a bicycle? What do you think they are used for? Wheels with "teeth," usually called gears, are another way to make it easier to move things or to change the direction of the movement. Here's an experiment to show how gears work.

You Will Need:

✓ 4 gears and a base (e.g. those made by Lego)
✓ paper
✓ pen

1 First arrange two gears next to each other on the base so one wheel turns the other one. Turn the first one in a clockwise direction. In which way does the second gear turn — the same way or the opposite direction?

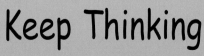

2 Predict which way you think a third gear will turn if it is placed so it can be turned by the second one. Test to find out if you are right.

3 Predict which way a fourth gear would turn if it was added next to the third one. Test again to find out.

Keep Thinking

This clock uses gears to move the hands. Which hand needs to move faster, the hour hand or the minute hand?

4 On a piece of paper, draw four circles next to each other to represent the gears. Draw arrows on each one to show the direction it turned. Can you see the pattern in the directions of the turns?

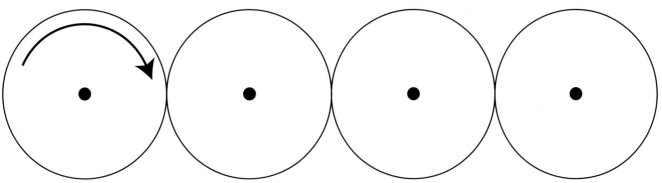

Don't Stop There

Take two gears that are different sizes, one large and one small. Place them onto the base so that one can turn the other. Put a mark on each wheel so you can count how many turns each one goes around. Turn the large wheel. What do you notice about how the small wheel turns? Does it turn at the same speed, faster, or slower than the large gear?

In Action

This hand-held drill uses two gears connected to each other to move the drill bit. The handle turns the large, upright gear. This turns the small gear that then turns the drill bit. The small gear turns much faster than the larger one, spinning the drill bit so that it screws into the wood.

Pull Together

DO YOU THINK YOU ARE very strong? Try this experiment and amaze your friends as you use a simple machine called a pulley. Pulleys spread the force over a longer distance to give you super strength!

1 Attach a long length of string to one curtain ring with a tight knot, and pass the end of the string through the other ring.

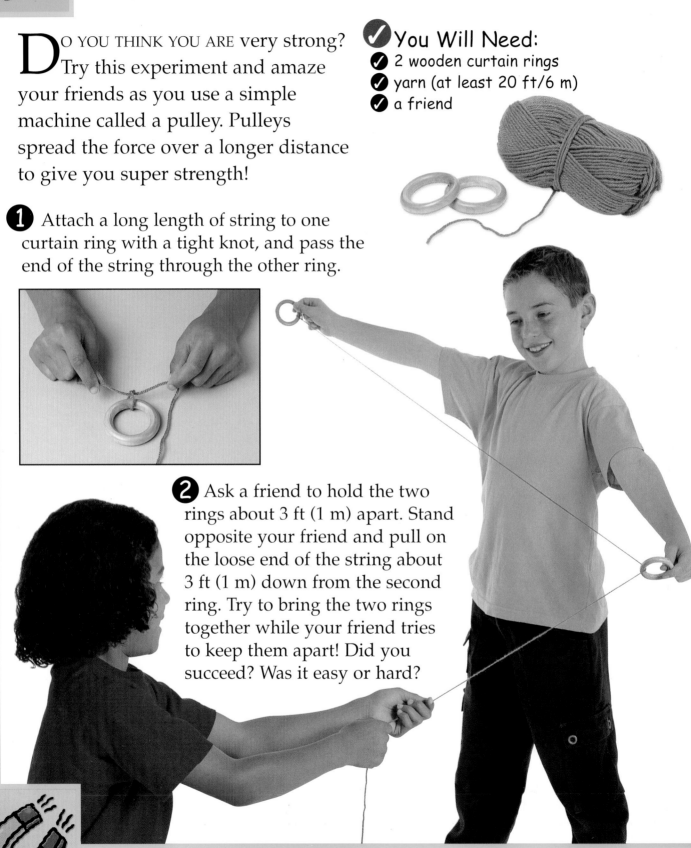

2 Ask a friend to hold the two rings about 3 ft (1 m) apart. Stand opposite your friend and pull on the loose end of the string about 3 ft (1 m) down from the second ring. Try to bring the two rings together while your friend tries to keep them apart! Did you succeed? Was it easy or hard?

3 Now pass the string in and out of the rings five times. Do you think it will be easier or harder to pull the rings together this time? Repeat the experiment with your friend holding the rings the same distance apart as before and find out. Do you have super strength?

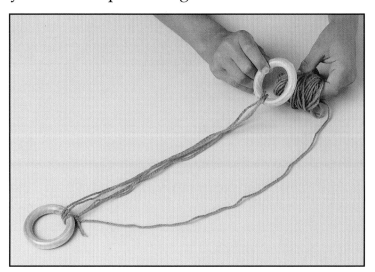

In Action

This mountain rescue team is using rope and pulleys to rescue someone from the side of a cliff. The pulleys help lift up the heavy bodies of the climbers.

Don't Stop There

● Pass the string through the rings ten times. Do you think it will be even easier to pull the rings together now? Repeat the experiment to find out.
● Ask your friend to hold up the ring with the loose end of string and attach a gym bag full of equipment to the other ring. Pull the end of the string to lift the bag with your pulley. Change the number of the loops in the string as before and see what happens.

Keep Thinking

How do you think pulleys are used to open and close curtains?

Pull It Up

WE USE PULLEYS IN MANY ways in daily life. In the last experiment you made your own pulley. Now use a store-bought pulley and find out more about how these simple machines make lifting easier.

✓ **You Will Need:**
- ✓ 2 kitchen chairs (or similar)
- ✓ a broom
- ✓ string (about 6 1/2 ft/2 m)
- ✓ a large bunch of keys
- ✓ a pulley (from hardware/craft stores)

1 Stand the chairs back to back about 3 ft (1 m) apart and lay the broom across the backs of the two chairs.

2 Tie the string to the loop at the top of the pulley and hook the keys onto the bottom of the pulley. Pass the string over the handle of the broom. Pull the loose end of string and lift the keys. Are they easy to lift up?

3 So far the pulley has not been used as a pulley. Now wind the string around the pulley and back over the broom handle. How do you think it will feel to lift the keys this time — easier, harder, or just the same?

4 To find out, pull the loose end of the string down. Did adding the pulley make your task easier? Do you think that the broom handle also acts as a pulley?

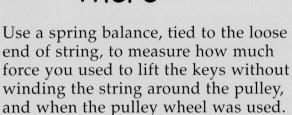

Don't Stop There

Use a spring balance, tied to the loose end of string, to measure how much force you used to lift the keys without winding the string around the pulley, and when the pulley wheel was used.

In Action

Cranes use pulleys to lift the heaviest of weights. They use several pulleys together and strong steel cable.

Keep Thinking

When you used a pulley, you needed to pull more string over a longer distance than when you just passed the string over the handle. Did you pull more string over a longer distance to give you super strength in the experiment on pages 22 and 23? If so, why?

What a Drag!

WHEN THE EGYPTIANS BUILT the pyramids thousands of years ago, they probably built long slopes to drag the huge stones up to the top instead of lifting them straight up. Discover more about the simple machine called a slope (or ramp) in this experiment.

✓ You Will Need:
- ✓ plank of wood (about 5 ft/1.5 m long)
- ✓ kitchen chair
- ✓ spring balance (to measure forces between 0 and 30 newtons)
- ✓ large toy truck or car
- ✓ tape measure

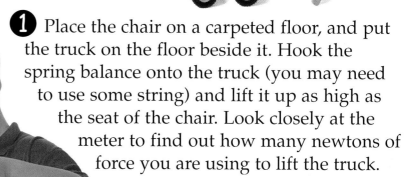

❶ Place the chair on a carpeted floor, and put the truck on the floor beside it. Hook the spring balance onto the truck (you may need to use some string) and lift it up as high as the seat of the chair. Look closely at the meter to find out how many newtons of force you are using to lift the truck.

	Distance truck traveled in in/cm	Force used in newtons
Straight up from the floor		
Along the slope		

❷ Record your result in a chart like the one shown.

❸ How far did the truck move when you lifted it? Use the tape measure to find out. Add this distance to the chart.

4 Now lean the plank of wood against the chair seat to make a slope. Place the truck at the slope's bottom. Hook the spring balance onto it as before and use it to pull the truck gently up the slope. Does it feel easier to pull this time? Read the spring balance to see how much force you are using. Add this to the chart.

5 Measure how far the truck traveled this time, and add your results to the chart.

6 Use your results chart to answer these questions. When you pulled up the truck, which way used less force — lifting it straight up or pulling it along a slope? In which way did the truck move the farthest? What does this tell you about using slopes to lift heavy objects?

Don't Stop There

Cut a right-angle triangle from a piece of thick felt material. Tape a pencil to one side of the right-angle and roll the felt around the pencil. Look closely at the edge of the felt as it winds around. Can you see that a screw is really a "wrapped-around slope?"

In Action

This road zigzagging up the hill makes it easier for vehicles to climb the hill than just going straight up.

Twisting Strength

PULLEYS ARE NOT THE ONLY simple machines that give you super strength. A screw spreads your force over a longer distance and "magnifies" your strength, too — the screw on a jack can even let you lift up a car! Find out more about screws in this experiment.

✓ You Will Need:
- ✓ a screw-type nutcracker
- ✓ some nuts e.g. walnuts (or a similar sized ball of pretzel dough if you have a nut allergy)
- ✓ a coin a little wider than the nut
- ✓ a felt-tip pen
- ✓ tape measure
- ✓ string

1 Place the coin on top of the nut, and use one hand to press down hard on it. Did you crack the nut? Was it easy to crack?

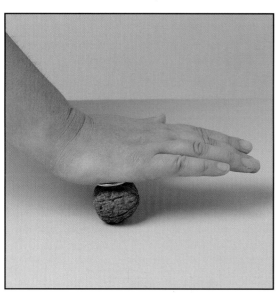

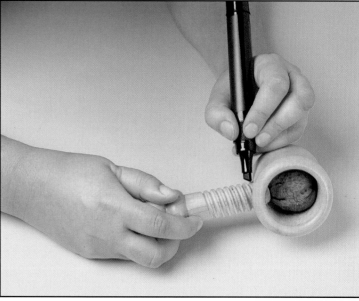

2 Take another nut and put it into the nutcracker. Twist the screw so it just touches the nut. Put a small mark on the thread of the screw where it reaches the nut holder.

Keep Thinking
How many different things can you think of that use a screw mechanism? Can you think of five? Ten? What tasks do these screws make easier?

3 Slowly turn the handle to twist the screw down on the nut until it cracks. Was it easy to crack this time? Put another mark on the screw thread to show how far the screw had moved.

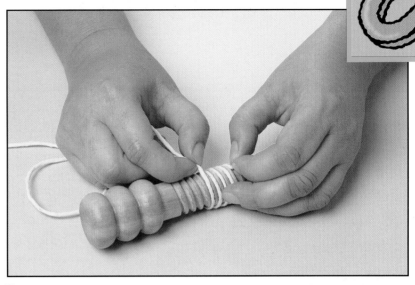

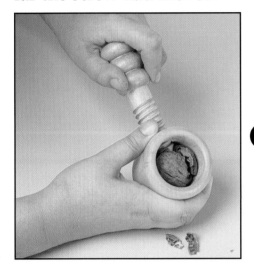

4 Wind the string around the screw from the first mark to the second mark and measure this distance to find how far the screw had to move to crack the nut. Is it farther than you expected? How has the distance the screw moved helped you crack the nut?

Don't Stop There

• Turn a faucet on. Try to stop the flow of water by pressing against the outlet with one hand! Was it possible? Now turn the faucet to stop the flow. Did you know that there is a screw mechanism inside it? Turning off the faucet tightens the screw and gradually stops the water.

• Watch an adult lift up a car with a jack and ask him or her to measure the distance the screw moves, just as you did with the nutcracker.

In Action

The screw mechanism on this G-clamp holds two pieces of wood together much more tightly than you could in your hands.

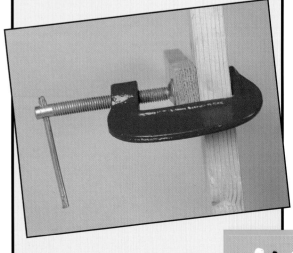

Glossary

This glossary gives the meaning of each word as it is used in this book.

Axle A cylindrical rod that passes through the center of a wheel and around which the wheel turns.

Belt drive A machine that uses a belt, such as an elastic band, stretched around rollers or wheels to move something.

Diameter The straight line from one edge of a circle to the other, passing through its center.

Dowel wood Thin, cylindrical rod of wood.

Drawbridge A bridge found in some medieval castles, usually across the castle's moat. A drawbridge could be raised by winches to stop enemies from entering the castle.

Effort The force applied to one part of a lever to lift a load.

Experiment A fair test done to find out more about something or to answer a question. Sometimes called an investigation.

Fair test A scientific test to find an accurate result. To keep the test fair, when you are experimenting, only one part (variable) must be changed and all the other parts (variables) must stay the same.

First-class lever A lever that has the fulcrum between the effort and the load.

Force A force is a push, a pull, or a twist. When a force acts on an object it makes it move, speed up, slow down, change direction, or change shape.

Fulcrum The point around which a lever pivots (turns) and is supported. Sometimes called a pivot.

Gear A wheel with "teeth" around its edge.

G-clamp A device shaped like the letter G which uses a screw-mechanism to hold, or clamp, two objects together.

Hinge A joint on which a door can swing to open and close.

Jack A screw-based mechanism used to lift the wheel of a vehicle off the ground in order to change the tire. We sometimes say you "jack" up the car.

Lever A simple machine used to lift or move a load, or to open something, in which a rigid bar turns around a fulcrum. There are three types of lever: first-class, second-class, and third-class.

Load The object lifted or moved by a lever. The load can sometimes be the "bar" of the lever itself, for example a door.

Machine A device that makes a task easier.

Mechanism Another word for machine, or working part of a large machine.

Newton (n) The standard unit used to measure force, named after the scientist Isaac Newton.

Pivot The point on which a lever is supported and around which it turns. Also called a fulcrum.

Predict To guess what will happen in an experiment before doing it.

Pulley A simple machine used to lift things or pull things together, usually by using thread or rope wrapped around a pulley wheel or wheels.

Pulley wheel A wheel with a groove on the outside rim for string or rope to move over, keeping it in position.

Ramp See Slope.

Result(s) The outcome of an experiment.

Screw A type of slope. It is used to fasten, lift, or squash things. It is a cylinder or cone with a spiral groove (the slope) cut into it.

Second-class lever A lever that has the load between the effort and the fulcrum.

Slope A slope is a simple machine that helps us move things up and down. It is surface (or plane) that goes gradually upwards or downwards. Also called an inclined plane or ramp.

Spring balance A device with a spring inside it that is used to measure force. The greater the force, the more the spring stretches.

Third-class lever A lever where the effort is between the fulcrum and the load.

Well A deep hole dug into the ground used to obtain water from deep beneath the ground.

Wheel A simple machine in which a circular frame or disk turns around an axle.

Winch A simple machine that winds string or rope around a wheel in order to lift a load.

Index

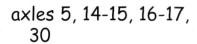